TABLE OF CONTENTS

Alive in Him

Learning to Live Abundantly in Christ

"I am come that they might have life,
and that they might have it more abundantly"
(John 10:10).

Alive in Him

Learning to Live Abundantly in Christ

"I am come that they might have life,
and that they might have it more abundantly"
(John 10:10).

Bonnie Peacock
Mary Loudermilk
Gwyn Oakes

Introduction

As with any new undertaking, there is so much to be learned when one makes the decision to live for Christ. When you are facing so much at once where do you turn?

This book is intended to be used as an introduction to communication and communion with God. That's what *Alive in Him* is all about. This collection of Scripture verses and Bible-based thoughts will sharpen your focus on the real issues of life—spiritual matters of personal importance. You will find relevant topics, each packed with God's ultimate truth.

Brief introductions enhance each section, which makes this a guidebook to refer to again and again. We pray that you will find insightful information on how to build up and reinforce your relationship with God. Each topic opens up at least one new truth or biblical principle about how God wants us to live.

With God's Word as your guide, you can't go wrong in the life ahead.

Gwyn Oakes
Ladies Ministries President
United Pentecostal Church International

A New You!

An Introduction to Your New Life in Christ

"Therefore if any man be in Christ, he is a new creature:
old things are passed away;
behold, all things are become new" (II Corinthians 5:17).

I have a new beginning

When you begin to walk with God, life starts all over. In fact, another term for *salvation* is "born again." (See John 3:1-7.) You are given a clean slate. Your past is behind, and a new life unfolds.

Just as if you had relocated to another country, everything around you is new and exciting. Being a child of God is a joy-filled privilege.

God is your heavenly Father, and you are His child. The people you worship with are your brothers and sisters.

The Bible is literally the words of God. Historical events are recounted to reveal how big He is as well as His thoughts and priorities. Practical insights into living are laid out.

The relationship that you have begun is one of love. Love is a two-way commitment. You read and obey God's Word and reap the many promises and benefits of being His child!

> "For this is the love of God, that we keep his commandments: and his commandments are not grievous" (I John 5:3).

Just as a parent knows what is best for his child, He too has your best interest at heart. When you walk with God and obey His Word, all things work together for your good. (See Romans 8:28.) He has promised. It is "impossible for God to lie" (Hebrews 6:18). You can trust Him.

Can I really talk to Him?

Yes! You can actually talk to God. He longs to hear your voice.

Remember—you are His child. (See II Corinthians 6:16-18.)

> *Parents may be in a crowded room, separated from their child and surrounded by chatter and laughter. Although many children are present, the parents immediately recognize the cry of their child.*

That is how God works too. He delights in His children. (See Proverbs 8:30.) Talking to God and listening to His voice as He speaks to your spirit is called "prayer."

God loves to be loved. He enjoys being thanked for the gifts that He gives each day. He wants to share your life. You can reveal your innermost secrets to Him.

It is important to set aside specific times each day to talk to God. If possible, find a quiet place. Bring your Bible, a pen, and paper. Make notes of exciting things that He shows you when you talk to Him and read His Word.

Your relationship with God is much more than the time you spend on your knees in prayer. You can communicate with Him all through the day. You will find that His presence enriches your life and brings peace and focus to all that you do.

"Thou wilt keep him in perfect peace, whose mind is stayed on thee: because he trusteth in thee" (Isaiah 26:3).

Prayer is the key to success.

Prayer is to the Christian what oxygen is to the body. While prayer is simply talking to God, a few strategies will multiply the effectiveness of your prayers.

"And this is the confidence that we have in him, that, if we ask any thing according to his will, he heareth us: And if we know that he hear us, whatsoever we ask, we know that we have the petitions that we desired of him" (I John 5:14-15).

When you pray, believe that God has heard your prayers and is working on your behalf. To believe is to expect.

"And all things, whatsoever ye shall ask in prayer, believing, ye shall receive" (Matthew 21:22).

Pray about *everything*! Be thankful for what God has done for you and what you believe He will do. Turn every anxiety into a prayer. While worry is depleting, prayer will lift you above the gloom and stress of life.

> "Be careful [anxious] for nothing; but in every thing by prayer and supplication with thanksgiving let your requests be made known unto God" (Philippians 4:6).

It is possible to pray consistently, everywhere, and in every situation. (See I Thessalonians 5:17.)

A prayer, in the name of Jesus, is just as powerful whispered under your breath in a room full of people as it is while on your knees in the prayer room.

"What does prayer do for me personally?" you might ask. Prayer does as much for the person praying as it does for the problems, people, and situations that require prayer.

As you pray, the Holy Spirit will often take control of your tongue, and you will find yourself once again speaking in an unknown language. Each time you speak in tongues, it is a beautiful experience.

> "Likewise the Spirit also helpeth our infirmities [weaknesses]: for we know not what we should pray for as we ought: but the Spirit itself maketh intercession for us" (Romans 8:26).

Not only does the Holy Ghost help us to pray for things that we do not know how to address, but prayer itself is an act of obedience. All through the Scriptures, obedience to God pays great dividends.

> "Your heavenly Father knoweth that ye have need of all these things. But seek ye first the kingdom of God, and his righteousness; and all these things shall be added unto you" (Matthew 6:32-33).

Prayer is powerful. Prayer works!

Doesn't it feel good to be clean?

The wonderful feeling that enveloped you when you repented of your sins can be enjoyed time and again. It is the plan of God that you daily bring your sins and problems to Him.

> "If we confess our sins, he is faithful and just to forgive us our sins, and to cleanse us from all unrighteousness" (I John 1:9).

When God forgives, He forgets. He is not like us. We may say that we forgive someone but be unable to forget the painful event. However, when the devil reminds you of past mistakes and you again repent, God no longer remembers what you did. Your past has been forgiven and forgotten.

> "He hath not dealt with us after our sins; nor rewarded us according to our iniquities. For as the heaven is high above the earth, so great is his mercy toward them that fear him. As far as the east is from the west, so far hath he removed our transgressions from us" (Psalm 103:10-12).

There is no sin too big or too bad that God will not forgive. His blood can cover everything. It is best to repent quickly. As soon as you realize that you have done or said something that is not pleasing to God, make it right and keep that beautiful feeling of CLEAN!

The family name is important.

At birth, every child is automatically given their family's name. It may be ordinary or bring privileges, power, and wealth. While your last name is still "Smith" or "Jones," when you are baptized in the name of Jesus, you also take on His name.

> "Then Peter said unto them, Repent, and *be baptized every one of you in the name of Jesus Christ* for the remission of sins, and ye shall receive the gift of the Holy Ghost" (Acts 2:38, emphasis added).

Baptism is an essential part of the plan of salvation. Your sins have been washed away, and you become a part of God's family. Tremendous power is available through the name of Jesus.

> "And Jesus came and spake unto them, saying, All power is given unto me in heaven and in earth" (Matthew 28:18).

Once given His name, you immediately are heir to your spiritual family's estate. Some benefits and privileges come with maturity; however, a multitude of doors are opened to you at "birth." At the name of Jesus your sins are washed away. You can use His name to defend and protect yourself. His name can be called in prayer and amazing things will happen.

"And whatsoever ye do in word or deed, do all in the name of the Lord Jesus" (Colossians 3:17).

God! Inside of me?

The Holy Ghost is the Spirit of God. Once you have repented of your sins and been baptized in Jesus' name, you are promised the gift of the Holy Ghost. (See Acts 2:38.)

"And we have known and believed the love that God hath to us. God is love; and he that dwelleth in love dwelleth in God, and God in him" (I John 4:16).

When you are filled with the Holy Ghost, God resides within you. What a thought. God! Inside of me? What a privilege.

You become a place where God lives. You are His tabernacle. You are his dwelling place.

"Know ye not that ye are the temple of God, and that the Spirit of God dwelleth in you?" (I Corinthians 3:16).

Knowing this, life takes on new meaning. The Spirit of God is with you in everything you say, everywhere you go, and everything you do.

The Holy Ghost is your Comforter and so much more. (See John 14:16-18.) When God resides within you, you will come to know and understand the things of the Spirit. Having the Spirit of God within you is an exciting way to live.

> "Howbeit when he, the Spirit of truth, is come, he will guide you into all truth ... and he will shew you things to come" (John 16:13).

God's Word is a road map for life.

Life is complicated. Read the directions. God did not save you and then leave you to fend for yourself. He provided His Word. The pages of the Bible hold the solutions to the dilemmas of life.

Wouldn't it be nice to know the answers to life's questions? The uncertainties of life are many. *If God would only speak to me!*

He does. The Word of God is the voice of God talking directly to you. (See John 1:1.) When you read the Bible, He speaks to your heart and mind. It is important to be prayerful when reading His Word.

> "Thy word is a lamp unto my feet, and a light unto my path" (Psalm 119:105).

The Word of God casts a light before you. A lamp is not a spotlight that illuminates a great distance, but it does reveal where to place your foot for your next step. Once you have taken that step, the lamp then casts its glow a bit further, allowing you to see the next few feet.

> "The grass withereth, the flower fadeth: but the word of our God shall stand for ever" (Isaiah 40:8).

God's Word does not change with the seasons, fashion, or political opinions. While things around you are continually changing, God and His Word are constant.

Not only can you read the Word of God, you can also apply it to your life and circumstances. It is a powerful tool that can be used every day. (See Hebrews 4:12.)

What happens now?

Living for God is exciting. Your old way of thinking is gradually replaced with new thoughts. Before, you may have struggled with feelings of low self-esteem or negativity. That can and will change.

You no longer walk alone, but God is with you, helping you through each day. As you read His Word, you begin to see things from His perspective. It will affect the way you think and speak.

> "And be not conformed to this world: but be ye transformed by the renewing of your mind, that ye may prove what is that good, and acceptable, and perfect, will of God" (Romans 12:2).

A good example of this wonderful change is when circumstances are overwhelming. Before knowing God you may have been inclined to complain, worry, and fret. Now, you can be confident in God's promises.

Here are some promises from God's Word:

- "It shall be well with them that fear God" (Ecclesiastes 8:12).
- "God is our refuge and strength, a very present help in trouble" (Psalm 46:1).
- "My grace is sufficient for thee" (II Corinthians 12:9).
- "No weapon that is formed against thee shall prosper" (Isaiah 54:17).
- "I will never leave thee, nor forsake thee. So that we may boldly say, The Lord is my helper" (Hebrews 13:5-6).

Change takes time. Don't be impatient or discouraged. We are all a work in progress. Remember, you have the Holy Ghost— God lives in you, and He will help you.

Guard your heart.

Just as eating wholesome foods, getting enough sleep, and exercising regularly are important for healthy bodies, feasting on God's Word, spending time in His presence, and attending church regularly are necessary for spiritual well-being.

Do not be surprised when your taste for entertainment and reading material changes. The Holy Ghost will help you to know what is good, clean, and beneficial for you.

"The peace of God, which passeth all understanding, shall keep your hearts and minds through Christ Jesus ... Whatsoever things are true, honest, just, pure, lovely, of good report ... if there be any virtue or praise, think on these things!" (Philippians 4:7-8, paraphrased).

You will occasionally slip into your old habits; a simple, but sincere, prayer of repentance puts you back in good standing with God. His Word tells us that He is "faithful and just to forgive us" (I John 1:9).

God honors every effort that you make to please Him.

> "Keep thy heart with all diligence; for out of it are the issues of life" (Proverbs 4:23).

Why is attending church important?

> "Not forsaking the assembling of ourselves together" (Hebrews 10:25).

Regular church attendance is extremely important. Every time the people of God gather to worship, He is present.

> "For where two or three are gathered together in my name, there am I in the midst of them" (Matthew 18:20).

Each time the minister of God teaches or preaches, you will learn nuggets of truth that you either need now or will need in the future. God knows the circumstances and problems of each person present and orchestrates every service to help, lift, and encourage.

Also, spending time with others who are walking with God is vital for growth. We need each other. So much can be learned from our brothers and sisters. While God answers the prayers of individuals, much more can be accomplished when several believers agree in prayer.

> "If two of you shall agree on earth as touching any thing that they shall ask, it shall be done for them of my Father which is in heaven" (Matthew 18:19).

There is strength in numbers.

> "A threefold cord is not quickly broken" (Ecclesiastes 4:12).

What is everyone excited about?

You may or may not be familiar with Pentecostal worship. There are biblical reasons for the way we worship God.

- "I will therefore that men pray every where, lifting up holy hands, without wrath and doubting" (I Timothy 2:8).

- "Let them praise his name in the dance: let them sing praises unto him with the timbrel and harp" (Psalm 149:3).

- "And now shall my head be lifted up above mine enemies round about me: therefore will I offer in his tabernacle sacrifices of joy; I will sing, yea, I will sing praises unto the LORD" (Psalm 27:6).

- "O clap your hands, all ye people; shout unto God with the voice of triumph" (Psalm 47:1)

Although health restraints and personality issues may affect the way we worship God, no one is exempt. God expects everyone to praise and worship Him.

You may notice that during any particular service some people weep and others laugh. Many wave their arms and others run, jump, dance, and shout.

It is important that we participate. We usher in the presence of God when we magnify His name. God inhabits praise. (See Psalm 22:3.) He is looking for those who will worship Him.

> "But the hour cometh, and now is, when the true worshippers shall worship the Father in spirit and in truth: for the Father seeketh such to worship him" (John 4:23).

> "Let every thing that hath breath praise the LORD. Praise ye the LORD" (Psalm 150:6).

What is faith?

Faith is simply a belief in God and what He can do. God responds to faith. In the life of a Christian, faith is a must!

> "But without faith it is impossible to please him: for he that cometh to God must believe that he is, and that he is a rewarder of them that diligently seek him" (Hebrews 11:6).

Faith is like a muscle. It has to be exercised to grow and develop. When faith is added to prayer, miracles happen, lives are changed, and situations are transformed.

When faith is added to words, they become the springboard for the impossible. Hope is born. Words of faith are powerful.

When faith is added to your thoughts, you can soar above your circumstances. Hope is restored. When faith is added, it transports you beyond the impossible into the realm of the supernatural.

> "Have faith in God. For verily I say unto you, That whosoever shall say unto this mountain, Be thou removed, and be thou cast into the sea; and shall not doubt in his heart, but shall believe that those things which he saith shall come to pass; he shall have whatsoever he saith. Therefore I say unto you, What things soever ye desire, when ye pray, believe that ye receive them, and ye shall have them" (Mark 11:22-24).

You are God's Ambassador.

You are an ambassador (II Corinthians 5:18-20). As part of God's kingdom, you represent Him to everyone you meet. You are known as belonging to God by your love for others, attitude of faith, and clean way of living. Your joy, peace, and love are qualities that everyone longs to possess.

> "A new commandment I give unto you, That you love one another; as I have loved you, that ye also love one

another. By this shall all men know that ye are my
disciples, if ye have love one to another"
(John 13:34-35).

The world is full of hurting people who are looking for Jesus.
Everywhere you go, you are an example of a Christian. Tell your
friends and family about what Jesus has done for you.

> "And he said unto them, Go ye into all the world, and
> preach the gospel to every creature" (Mark 16:15).

It is not necessary to know all the answers before telling others
about God. The best way to bring someone else to the Lord is
simply to tell them what happened to you. Others can help you
answer questions when they arise.

> "Go home to thy friends, and tell them how great things
> the Lord hath done for thee, and hath had compassion
> on thee" (Mark 5:19).

You are significant.

You are important to God and to your new church family. God
has a special role for you to play in His kingdom that can only be
filled by you.

> "For I know the thoughts that I think toward you, saith
> the LORD, thoughts of peace, and not of evil, to give you
> an expected end" (Jeremiah 29:11).

When God saved you, He had a plan. When He equipped you with all your interests, talents, abilities, and dreams, it was for a significant purpose.

> "Thus saith the LORD that made thee, and formed thee from the womb, which will help thee; Fear not ... thou ... whom I have chosen" (Isaiah 44:2).

There is a place for everyone in God's house. Every member is important in His family. Although each person fulfills different roles, no one believer is more valuable than another.

The church exists to help you and is excited that you have become a part of the family of God.

How to Be
Filled with God's Spirit
God's Plan Is for Everyone

**"I am come that they might have life,
and that they might have it more abundantly" (John 10:10).**

A desire exists in every heart to be at peace with God, to be saved.

- What does it mean to be saved?

Salvation is a fresh start—a chance to be born all over again. It is a life-changing, beautiful experience and our birth into the family of God.

- But is it possible for just anyone to be saved?
- How do we know we are saved?

In the New Testament, others had questions too: "What shall we do?" (Acts 2:37).

The answer was simple. "Repent, and be baptized every one of you in the name of Jesus Christ for the remission of sins, and ye shall receive the gift of the Holy Ghost" (Acts 2:38).

Centuries later, men and women are still repenting of their sins, being baptized in Jesus' name, and receiving the gift of the Holy Ghost! In fact, "The promise is unto you, and to your children, and to all that are afar off, even as many as the Lord our God shall call" (Acts 3:39).

The new birth experience is for everyone. "The Lord is ... not willing that any should perish, but that all should come to repentance" (II Peter 3:9). An open invitation is extended to every man, woman, boy, and girl: "Come. And let him that heareth say, Come. And let him that is athirst come. And whosoever will, let him take the water of life freely" (Revelation 22:17).

The plan of salvation is not optional. When Jesus walked on earth, He told Nicodemus. "Except a man be born of water and of the Spirit, he cannot enter into the kingdom of God" (John 3:5). No one can be saved without being born again.

Three steps are vital to this new-birth salvation experience: repentance, water baptism in Jesus' name, and receiving the gift of the Holy Ghost. Let's take a few moments to see what the Scriptures say about each.

1.   Repentance

We are all sinners in need of a Savior. The psalmist admitted, "I was shapen in iniquity; and in sin did my mother conceive me" (Psalm 51:5). From the fall of man in the Garden of Eden, the sin problem has been mankind's biggest struggle.

God hates sin but loves the sinner. "Except ye repent, ye shall all likewise perish" (Luke 13:3). Left to our own devices, none of us would ever be saved. God, though, provided a way for us to live throughout eternity with Him. Not only does salvation ensure our destination when we die, but it establishes an intimate relationship between us and God that we can enjoy throughout our lives!

This relationship is important to God. He loved us enough to come to earth and die for our salvation. "For God so loved the world, that he gave his only begotten Son, that whosoever believeth in him should not perish, but have everlasting life" (John 3:16).

The Scriptures tell us that He was "bruised for our iniquities" (Isaiah 53:5). Christ died to take away the sin of the whole world. (See John 1:29.) That includes our sin too!

Repentance is easy. The only requirements are a sincere heart and sorrow for past mistakes. When we repent, we turn away from our old, sinful lifestyle and begin to walk in a new direction. Let us pray:

Dear Lord, thank You for being the lamb that was slain to take away my sin. Forgive me for every thought, word, and action that displeases You. Create in me a clean heart and place a right spirit within me. I want to live for You. I want to please You with my life. I accept Your forgiveness. In Jesus' name. Amen. (See Psalm 51:10.)

It is important to receive or accept God's forgiveness. Although we may remember our misdeeds, God has forgiven and forgotten!

2.   Baptism in Jesus' name

"Neither is there salvation in any other: for there is none other name under heaven given among men, whereby we must be saved" (Acts 4:12).

The next step in the plan of salvation is water baptism. While God forgives our sins when we repent, water baptism in Jesus' name washes them away. We are submerged in water and rise again to walk as a brand new creature.

"As far as the east is from the west, so far hath he removed our transgressions from us" (Psalm 103:12).

Although we can still remember our past and Satan tries to tell us we are unworthy of God's love and mercy, we know our sin is gone. In fact, it is under Christ's blood. The blood Christ shed on Calvary purchased the remission of our sin.

Baptism in the name of Jesus places us in the family of God. While our name remains the same, we now have the name of Jesus applied to our life. We are His child, and we have a place in His kingdom.

The name of Jesus is powerful. We can use His name to defend ourselves. It is important to pray in Jesus' name.

"And Jesus came and spake unto them, saying, All power is given unto me in heaven and in earth" (Matthew 28:18).

3.   The Gift of the Holy Ghost

This last step in the salvation process is exciting. While we experience a beautiful cleansing when we repent and are baptized in Jesus' name, speaking in tongues as we receive the gift of the Holy Ghost is the proof we are saved.

What is the Holy Ghost?

The New Testament tells of Christ's birth, life, ministry, death, and resurrection. When He walked on earth He touched lives, healed the sick, raised the dead, and taught a new way of living. Before leaving His followers, Jesus gave them directions: "Tarry ye in the city of Jerusalem, until ye be endued with power from on high" (Luke 24:49).

And when the day of Pentecost was fully come, they were all with one accord in one place.

And suddenly there came a sound from heaven as of a rushing mighty wind, and it filled all the house where they were sitting.

And there appeared unto them cloven tongues like as of fire, and it sat upon each of them.

> And they were all filled with the Holy Ghost, and began
> to speak with other tongues, as the Spirit gave them
> utterance.
>
> (Acts 2:1-4)

Others were amazed at what they saw. One hundred and twenty people were speaking in languages they did not know, as the Spirit of God—the Holy Ghost—filled them to overflowing.

Today, when we are filled with the Holy Ghost, we too begin to speak in an unknown language. This unknown tongue is a sign—proof positive that we have been filled with the Spirit of God.

But how do we receive the Holy Ghost?

If we have repented of our sins, the Holy Ghost is for us. When we repent we are cleansed of the junk that has filled our lives. Our hearts are now empty containers, ready to be filled with the beautiful presence of God.

After repenting, we enjoy a glorious feeling of clean. It is natural to thank God for His forgiveness. We receive His love. As we return His love, focus on Him, thank Him, worship Him, and praise Him, He begins to fill us with His Spirit.

As we talk to God, our tongue may feel thick and our words may not sound distinct. How we sound is not important. As we continue worshiping and thanking God, He continues to fill us with His Spirit.

Imagine water filling a glass. The glass is filled higher and higher until the water begins to splash over. When we receive the Holy Ghost, the same thing happens. God's presence fills us until we cannot hold any more and we begin to speak in an unknown language.

This beautiful experience should be repeated often. Making a habit of praying in the Holy Ghost ensures a healthy, strong relationship with God. This experience never grows old. The longer we walk with God, the more real He becomes.

Now is a good time to begin. God is waiting. He is just as close as the mention of His name. Jesus.

Key points:

- It is possible to repent and receive the Holy Ghost alone. Baptism, however, requires assistance. Make sure the person who baptizes you believes in the New Testament, Book of Acts experience. Water immersion in the name of the Lord Jesus Christ is vital.

- The salvation plan does more than save us initially. It keeps us saved.

- Be quick to repent.

- Speak in tongues often. "The Spirit also helpeth our infirmities: for we know not what we should pray for as we ought: but the Spirit itself maketh intercession for us with groanings which cannot be uttered"

(Romans 8:26). When we don't know what to say or we feel wounded and depleted, the Holy Ghost will pray for things we do not know how to express, and it will restore us too!

The Lord's Prayer
A Beginner's Guide to Prayer

"He that cometh to God must believe that he is, and that he is a rewarder of them that diligently seek him" (Hebrews 11:6).

Have you ever wanted to talk to God but didn't know what to say?

We all have.

God is God. He is in heaven. We are—well—we are not God, and we reside on earth. How do we communicate with Him?

He knew we would have questions and gave us an outline of how to pray:

> But you, when you pray, go into your room, and when you have shut your door, pray to your Father who is in the secret place; and your Father who sees in secret will reward you openly.
>
> But when you pray, do not use vain repetitions as the heathen do. For they think that they will be heard for their many words.

Therefore do not be like them. For your Father knows the things you have need of before you ask Him.

In this manner, therefore, pray: Our Father in heaven, Hallowed be Your name.

Your kingdom come. Your will be done on earth as it is in heaven.

Give us this day our daily bread.

And forgive us our debts, as we forgive our debtors.

And do not lead us into temptation, but deliver us from the evil one. For Yours is the kingdom and the power and the glory forever. Amen.

(Matthew 6:6-13, New King James Version)

These verses are referred to as the "Lord's Prayer." They provide an example of how to approach God and the things we should pray about.

Let's explore each phrase individually:

1.   "Our Father in heaven"

Stop for a moment and think about the word "father." Our own experiences affect how we feel about fathers. While ours may have been wonderful, in our society fathers are sometimes absent, neglectful, or abusive.

God is not like any earthly father. He exceeds our wildest dreams and expectations. We did nothing to deserve this amazing relationship. It is difficult to understand how God can be our Father, but it was all His idea.

> "I will be a Father to you, and you shall be My sons and daughters, says the LORD Almighty" (II Corinthians 6:18, NKJV).

He made it possible for us to be born into His family, receive all the benefits of being in His kingdom, and enjoy a relationship with Him. We are precious to Him. (See Zechariah 2:8.)

2.   "Hallowed be Your name"

The word "hallow" means to honor as sacred or to consecrate. God is holy. He is without equal. He stands alone, a massive, awesome God. (See Isaiah 44:6; John 1:3.) We are to honor and respect Him. The Bible reveals different aspects of God's character. In the Old Testament, He was referred to as Jehovah. In different settings and situations new attributes of Jehovah God were revealed.

Jehovah-Jireh   Jehovah is our provider.
                           Genesis 22:7-14
Jehovah-Rophe   Jehovah is our healer.
                           Exodus 15:22-26
Jehovah-Nissi   Jehovah is our banner.
                           Exodus 17:15-16
Jehovah-M'Kaddesh   Jehovah sanctifies us.
                           Leviticus 20:7-8

Jehovah-Shalom	Jehovah is our peace.
	Judges 6:24
Jehovah-Tsidkenu	Jehovah our righteousness.
	Jeremiah 23:5-6
Jehovah-Rohi	Jehovah our shepherd.
	Psalm 23:1
Jehovah-Shammah	Jehovah is there.
	Ezekiel 48:35

The above two statements, "Our Father in heaven" and "Hallowed be Your name" provide a balance. He loves us more than we can comprehend, yet He is Almighty God and should be revered. This basic knowledge of God is important. We can be confident that He knows what is best for us and cares for us deeply.

> "And we know that all things work together for good to them that love God, to them who are the called according to his purpose" (Romans 8:28).

3. "Your kingdom come. Your will be done on earth as it is in heaven."

When we pray that God's will and purpose be done on earth, we are submitting our own will and agenda to Him. Because we know He loved us enough to give His life for our salvation and chose to become our Father, we can trust Him.

Every day we should pray that His will be done in

- every part of our lives;
- our family (spouse, children, and other family members);
- our church (pastor, leadership, faithfulness and victory of other believers);
- government (city, state, and national–judicial, legislative, and executive).

This pattern of prayer teaches us to make His kingdom a priority. When we pray that His will be done, we are placing God in His rightful place in our lives. It is all about Him!

4. "Give us this day our daily bread."

After establishing God as the focal point of our lives, we can take our concerns, needs, and desires to Him too. When we do things God's way, He will take care of us.

"But seek ye first the kingdom of God, and his righteousness; and all these things shall be added unto you" (Matthew 6:33).

We all desire God's blessings and need His provision. Several keys are instrumental in receiving from God.

- Make sure we are in the will of God (prayer life, faithfulness, work habits, and obedience in giving).

- Believe it is God's will to bless: "It is your Father's good pleasure to give you the kingdom" (Luke 12:32).
- Be specific.
- Be patient, knowing God has heard, He is working, and the answer is on the way!

5. "And forgive us our debts, as we forgive our debtors."

Forgiveness is not easy to give, but we all need to be recipients for we have all "sinned, and come short of the glory of God" (Romans 3:23). Perhaps that is why God tied the two together.

"And when ye stand praying, forgive, if ye have ought against any: that your Father also which is in heaven may forgive you your trespasses. But if ye do not forgive, neither will your Father which is in heaven forgive your trespasses" (Mark 11:25-26).

Pray daily:

- Ask God to forgive wrong thoughts, words, and deeds.
- Forgive those who have wronged us.
- Ask God to help us to have a forgiving attitude.

"Create in me a clean heart, O God; and renew a right spirit within me" (Psalm 51:10).

6. "And do not lead us into temptation, but deliver us from the evil one."

Another way to pray this statement is, "Lord, lead me not into trials, and deliver me from a bad attitude." Some problems and trials we bring on ourselves; others are divinely permitted for our growth and maturity.

We can pray:

- Lord, help me to learn character, maturity, and Christ-likeness without needing to go through adversity.

"My brethren, count it all joy when you fall into various trials, knowing that the testing of your faith produces patience. But let patience have its perfect work, that you may be perfect and complete, lacking nothing" (James 1:2-4, NKJV).

- Lord, help me to overcome the temptation of the evil one who steals, kills, and destroys. (See John 10:10.)

"There hath no temptation taken you but such as is common to man: but God is faithful, who will not suffer you to be tempted above that ye are able; but will with the temptation also make a way to escape, that ye may be able to bear it" (I Corinthians 10:13).

7. "For Yours is the kingdom and the power and the glory forever. Amen."

The kingdom, power, and glory all belong to God. He desires to be honored. Our prayers should begin and end with affirming our love and adoration for God. He is the Almighty God, our loving Father, and dearest Friend!

"The effectual fervent prayer of a righteous man availeth much" (James 5:16).

Key points:

- When you pray, believe that God hears you. He longs for you to talk to Him. As your Father, He wants to spend time with you.

- Remember that what matters to you matters to Him. He knows, cares, and understands.

- Prayer can be silent or said aloud.

- Pray in Jesus' name and with faith in His Word.

- Prayer is effective and powerful.

- Prayer establishes our relationship with God.

The Bible:
Our Guide for Daily Living
The Importance of God's Word in Our Lives

"Order my steps in thy word" (Psalm 119:133).

As we begin our brand new life in Christ, we are eager to learn more about walking in His way. God's Word says that we are a new person. We have changed; we are not the same person as before.

> "Therefore, if anyone is in Christ, he is a new creation; old things have passed away; behold, all things have become new" (II Corinthians 5:17, NKJV).

We have discovered the importance of prayer in our life from previous chapters of this book, but another equally essential habit to develop is that of consistently reading the Word of God each day. Just as it is important to eat well-balanced meals for physical health; the same is true for our spiritual well-being. We would never consider ourselves well fed if we ate a meal only once or twice each week. Neither do we stay strong spiritually if we take in the food of God's Word only occasionally.

God wants us to be successful in living for Him, so He has given us the Bible as a guide. From its pages we discover wonderful truths about how to live in a way that pleases Him. It also reveals things that will be harmful to our relationship with Him.

> "This Book of the Law shall not depart from your mouth, but you shall meditate in it day and night, that you may observe to do according to all that is written in it. For then you will make your way prosperous, and then you will have good success" (Joshua 1:8, NKJV).

As we hold the Bible in our hands, we may ask, "How can I ever understand all this? There is so much here! I don't even know where to start." It is no wonder we feel overwhelmed. The Bible is actually one large book which contains sixty-six smaller books within. These sixty-six books are divided into the Old Testament (thirty-nine books) and New Testament (twenty-seven books). Some books, such as the Psalms, are very long while others take barely a page and can be read in a single sitting.

II Timothy 3:16 tells us that the Bible "is given by inspiration of God." It is unlike any other book. Although it was written by many men over a period of thousands of years, all of the words were inspired by God. He guided their thoughts and ideas so that they were recording His thoughts. When we read the Bible, we are reading the words of the eternal God.

As we study God's Word, we begin to lay a foundation and gain understanding. When we learn the Word and make it part of our daily life, it keeps us steady and secure.

"The law of his God is in his heart; none of his steps shall slide" (Psalm 37:31).

Here are some of the things that God's Word does in our lives:

- Helps us understand what God wants us to do
- Helps us overcome temptations
- Gives us wisdom to deal with problems we face each day
- Gives us knowledge so that we can in turn teach others

There are simple steps that we can take to help us understand and grow in our knowledge of the Bible.

1.   Begin with prayer.

It is important to combine prayer with study of the Bible. We must ask God to open our heart to His Word and give us insight into the meaning of each passage as we study. Pray for understanding.

"The righteousness of Your testimonies is everlasting; Give me understanding, and I shall live."
(Psalm 119:144, NKJV).

"For the Lord gives wisdom; From His mouth come knowledge and understanding" (Proverbs 2:6, NKJV).

"The entrance of Your words gives light; It gives understanding to the simple" (Psalm 119:130, NKJV).

2.   Go to the source.

Many people read books about the Bible but do not read the Bible itself. It is important that we go directly to God's Word. As we compare one passage of scripture with another, we will discover that the Bible explains itself.

> "Search the scriptures; for in them ye think ye have eternal life: and they are they which testify of me" (John 5:39).

> "But his delight is in the law of the LORD; and in his law doth he meditate day and night" (Psalm 1:2).

3.   Accept the Bible as completely true.

Many consider the accounts within its pages as mere fables or interesting stories, but God's Word is absolutely true.

> "Thy word is true from the beginning: and every one of thy righteous judgments endureth for ever" (Psalm 119:160).

> "For ever, O LORD, thy word is settled in heaven" (Psalm 119:89).

> "But holy men of God spake as they were moved by the Holy Ghost" (II Peter 1:21).

4. Make a plan.

If new to studying the Word of God, begin by reading a book at a time. A good place to start is with the Gospels, which are the first four books of the New Testament. The Book of Luke is possibly the most complete story of the life of Jesus and His teachings. The Book of Acts, which follows the Gospels, tells the history of the beginning of the church.

Consistent study is essential to spiritual growth. There are many ways to study: by topic, by Bible character, by book, or by verse. (A concordance helps locate related verses easily.)

> "For whatever things were written before were written for our learning, that we through the patience and comfort of the Scriptures might have hope" (Romans 15:4, NKJV).

> "Be diligent to present yourself approved to God, a worker who does not need to be ashamed, rightly dividing the word of truth" (II Timothy 2:15, NKJV).

> "As newborn babes, desire the sincere milk of the word, that ye may grow thereby" (I Peter 2:2).

5. Make it personal.

Keep pen and paper at hand to write down any thoughts or impressions that come while studying. Note any questions that come to mind regarding the passage. Define key words and phrases to increase understanding. (A good Bible dictionary will help with this.)

As we study, it is good to ask ourselves these questions:

- **What does it say? What do I see?** (Observation)

- **What does it mean?** (Interpretation)

- **What does it mean to me personally?** (Application)

"Open thou mine eyes, that I may behold wondrous things out of thy law" (Psalm 119:18).

"O how love I thy law! It is my meditation all the day" (Psalm 119:97).

6. Apply the Word to daily life.

It is not enough just to study God's Word; we must also obey what is written—put what we have learned into practice.

"But be doers of the word, and not hearers only, deceiving yourselves. For if anyone is a hearer of the word and not a doer, he is like a man observing his natural face in a mirror; for he observes himself, goes away, and immediately forgets what kind of man he was" (James 1:22-24, NKJV).

"All scripture is given by inspiration of God, and is profitable for doctrine, for reproof, for correction, for instruction in righteousness" (II Timothy 3:16).

As we make God's Word a consistent part of our daily lives, we will grow in our Christian walk. It has been said that "many books inform, but the Bible transforms." We will be changed—transformed—to become more like our Lord. Our lives will be richer as we put His Word in our hearts.

"Let the word of Christ dwell in you richly" (Colossians 3:16).

Key Points:

- God has given us His Word so that we can successfully live for Him.

- Prayer combined with Bible reading will give us an understanding of God and His plan for us.

- We must accept the Bible as inspired and completely true.

- We must develop a plan to consistently study God's Word.

- It is important that we apply His Word to our daily lives.

The Power of Praying God's Word

A Guide for Gaining Victory through the Word of God

"Thy word is a lamp unto my feet, and a light unto my path"
(Psalm 119:105).

It is sometimes difficult to feel we have the right to ask God for anything. We know the Bible is true and that God loves others, but we are all too aware of our own flaws and failures.

Many voices surround us. Our mind has been programmed by our past experiences and influences. We are surrounded by the opinions of others, the media presents yet another view, and we have an enemy, Satan, who constantly tries to deceive us. God has given us His Word to give us help, hope, peace, and direction.

> "The words that I speak unto you, they are spirit, and they are life" (John 6:63).

We must make a point of knowing what the Word of God says. Unless we do, we will follow voices that lead us down a wrong path or nowhere at all.

When our minds are in turmoil and do not know how to pray, we can open the Bible and find God's promises. When we turn the verses of scripture into prayers, we strengthen our faith in His Word and serve the enemy notice that we belong to God—the enemys tricks and lies are not working!

It is important to remember that the enemy is as big and bad as he is going to get, but we are still growing! "Ye are of God, little children, and have overcome them: because greater is he that is in you, than he that is in the world" (I John 4:4).

The Word of God is alive. God speaks to us through the pages of the Bible. (See John 1:1.) Whatever we face, the answers are found in God's Word.

Let's take a look at a few examples:

When we are overwhelmed, the Word of God states, "I can do all things through Christ which strengtheneth me" (Philippians 4:13). When things happen we do not understand, we are reassured, "All things work together for good to them that love God, to them who are the called according to his purpose" (Romans 8:28).

Only through prayer can we be victorious. God's Word causes us to believe it will happen even before we see it done. When God's Word is part of our very being, we can then pray the Scriptures for things happening in our lives.

> "For the word of God is living and powerful, and sharper than any two-edged sword, piercing even to the division of soul and spirit, and of joints and marrow, and is a

discerner of the thoughts and intents of the heart"
(Hebrews 4:12, NKJV).

"For the weapons of our warfare are not carnal but
mighty in God for pulling down strongholds"
(II Corinthians 10:4, NKJV).

Below are selected Scripture verses for various subjects for
which we pray.

1.   Praying the Word for our children

Through prayer, parents receive wisdom to guide their children
in godly lifestyles. Praying for our child involves petitioning God
for His input into the fiber of the child's everyday life. God hears
the sincere and fervent prayers of parents.

> "But the mercy of the LORD is from everlasting to
> everlasting on those who fear Him, and His
> righteousness to children's children, to such as keep His
> covenant, and to those who remember His
> commandments to do them" (Psalm 103:17-18, NKJV).

Following are two examples of using Scripture verses to pray the
Word for your child. Look them up in the Bible and compare the
wording. As you study, you will find many more.

> "Be my child's hiding place and his shield; let him hope
> in Thy Word, oh Lord." (See Psalm 119:114.)

> "Be my child's light and his salvation; whom shall he

fear? Be the strength of his life, oh Lord; then of whom shall he be afraid? When the wicked, even his enemies, come upon him, let them stumble and fall. Though an army come against him, let him not fear; let him be confident in You, Lord." (See Psalm 27:1-3.)

2.   Salvation

Claim the following promises for your child:

"But thus saith the LORD, Even the captives of the mighty shall be taken away, and the prey of the terrible shall be delivered: for I will contend with him that contendeth with thee, and I will save thy children" (Isaiah 49:25).

When you personalize the Word, this verse becomes:

"Oh, Lord, you said that you would contend with those who contend with me and that you would save my children. I claim that promise according to Your Word."

Then personalize and claim the promises of the following verses:

- Acts 2:38-39
- Psalm 18:2
- Psalm 20:5-6
- Psalm 24:4-5
- Psalm 25:4-7
- Psalm 62:6-7

3.   Ownership

Pray that your child will take ownership of the faith at an accountable age and that it will become his faith, not just the faith of his parents.

Pray Psalm 119:11-16 the following way:

> "Help my child to hide Your Word in his heart so that he will not sin against You. For You will teach him Your principles. Help him declare with his own lips all the laws You have set. Help him to rejoice in Your Word as much as he would in riches. Help him to study Your commandments and have respect for Your ways. Help him delight in Your laws and not forget Your Word."

Now pray the following verses in the same manner.

- Proverbs 23:23
- I Timothy 6:12
- Psalm 25:5
- Proverbs 3:3-6

- Isaiah 26:3
- II Corinthians 13:8
- Matthew 17:20

4.   Health and protection

Pray Psalm 91:9-12 this way:

> "Dear Lord, please help my child to make You his refuge. Your Word promises that if he does, evil will not snare him. Give Your angels charge over him to keep

him in all Your ways—not just part of them, but all your ways, Lord. Let the angels bear him up in their hands and keep him from harm."

Continue by praying the following verses and others in the same manner.

- Isaiah 40:31
- II Corinthians 12:9
- Proverbs 18:10
- Deuteronomy 31:8
- Deuteronomy 33:27
- Psalm 34:17

5. Choosing friends

"Choose you this day whom ye will serve" (Joshua 24:15).

Pray the preceding verse this way:

"Help not only my family but also help me to serve and trust in You, and direct us in choosing the right friends."

- Matthew 6:33
- Philippians 4:8
- II Corinthians 6:14
- Ephesians 5:11

"As he [Elijah] was going up by the way, there came forth little children ... and mocked him, and said unto him, Go up, thou bald head; go up, thou bald head. And he turned back, and looked on them, and cursed them. ... And there came forth two she bears out of the wood, and tare forty and two children of them" (II Kings 2:23-24).

Pray the preceding verse this way:

> "Help my child to understand that he should avoid a gang spirit and that these are not the types of groups to befriend. Help him to see by the examples in Your Word that wrong friends will destroy him."

> • Judges 16:30

6. Finding the will of God

> "But seek ye first the kingdom of God, and his righteousness; and all these things shall be added unto you" (Matthew 6:33).

Pray the preceding verse this way:

> "Lord, help my family and me to always seek Your kingdom and to serve You righteously. As our Creator, You have definite plans for our lives. Help us to understand that the steps of a good man are ordered by the Lord."

> • Jeremiah 29:11   • Psalm 144:12
> • Proverbs 3:5-6   • Romans 8:28
> • Philippians 4:6-7

7. Moral purity

> "Wherefore gird up the loins of your mind, be sober, and hope to the end for the grace that is to be brought unto

you at the revelation of Jesus Christ; as obedient children, not fashioning yourselves according to the former lusts in your ignorance: but as he which hath called you is holy, so be ye holy in all manner of conversation; because it is written, Be ye holy; for I am holy" (I Peter 1:13-16).

Pray this powerful passage in the following manner:

"Dear Lord, help us to bring our minds into subjection to You. Let us be sober in all things. Keep the revelation of who You are alive in our hearts and minds. Help us to do this as an obedient child would honor his parent. Stir our minds to remember that because You are holy, we must also be holy in appearance as well as in our hearts."

Continue in the same manner with the following verses.

- I Timothy 4:12
- Galatians 5:16
- Ephesians 4:22-24

- I Peter 2:11
- James 1:21-22
- Philippians 4:8

8. Spiritual understanding

"Shew me thy ways, O LORD; teach me thy paths. Lead me in thy truth, and teach me: for thou art the God of my salvation; on thee do I wait all the day" (Psalm 25:4-5).

Pray this:

> "Show us Your ways, Lord. Teach us the paths we should follow. Lead us in your truth. Help us to always wait on You for direction and awareness of right and wrong."

> * Psalm 32:8
> * Psalm 143:10
> * Proverbs 12:15
> * Isaiah 48:17
> * I Corinthians 2:14
> * II Thessalonians 3:3

9.   Future and career

Pray the following verses as promises from the Lord:

> "The steps of a good man are ordered by the LORD: and he delighteth in his way" (Psalm 37:23).

> * Jeremiah 29:11
> * Romans 12:2
> * Deuteronomy 5:27
> * Romans 8:37
> * Deuteronomy 10:12
> * Proverbs 24:27

10.   Financial blessings

> "But thou shalt remember the LORD thy God: for it is he that giveth thee power to get wealth, that he may establish his covenant which he sware unto thy fathers, as it is this day" (Deuteronomy 8:18).

Pray the following prayer for your family. Read the Scripture text before and after the above passage:

> "Dear Father, I thank You for the knowledge You have given me. Help me never to forget that it is You who gives me health and strength to work and provide for my financial welfare. Help me to be wise and through a holy lifestyle to claim Your promises. Thank You for helping me to understand that the work of Your kingdom must be first in my life. As I give to You, You will in turn give back to me. I know that You will provide my needs according to Your riches in glory so long as I obey You."

- Malachi 3:10-11
- Isaiah 48:17
- Deuteronomy 7:12-13
- Proverbs 3:9-10
- II Corinthians 9:7-8
- Proverbs 10:22
- Luke 6:38

11.   Future spouse

> "For I know the thoughts that I think toward you, saith the LORD, thoughts of peace and not of evil, to give you an expected end" (Jeremiah 29:11).

Pray Jeremiah's promise the following way for your child or for yourself:

> "I thank You, Lord, that I am in Your thoughts and that You have a definite plan for our lives. I ask that You send the spouse You have chosen for [my child/me] who will faithfully walk with You and invite peace and rest into the home through Your blessings and presence."

- Colossians 1:9-10
- Proverbs 4:14
- Proverbs 16:20

- Proverbs 31:10-12, 27-28
- Matthew 6:33
- Matthew 7:7-8

12. Prodigal child

"Fear not: for I am with thee: I will bring thy seed from the east, and gather thee from the west; I will say to the north, Give up; and to the south, Keep not back: bring my sons from far, and my daughters from the ends of the earth; even every one that is called by my name: for I have created him for my glory, I have formed him; yea, I have made him" (Isaiah 43:5-7).

Pray this awesome promise for your prodigal:

"Thank You, Lord, for the promise of Your Word. that I claim for my prodigal. You covered the four corners of the earth in the promise to Isaiah concerning Your children. I realize this was concerning the seed of Abraham, but through Your shed blood, we have become children of the promise! According to Your Word, Lord, wherever he is now—north, south, east, or west—honor Your Word and speak to his heart. In Your mercy, grant him space for repentance. Stir him with a desire to surrender his life to You. Help him to pray as King David, and create in him a clean heart and renew a right spirit within him. Just as You formed him, reform him now, I ask in Your name!"

In prayer, remind the Lord of the following precious promises:

- Matthew 7:7-8
- Isaiah 44:22
- Proverbs 20:7

- John 14:13-14
- Acts 2:39
- Isaiah 61:1-4

13. Praying the Word for your spouse

God desires for marriages to have intimacy of spirit, soul, and body. Usually couples need help most in developing spiritual intimacy. The foundation of becoming one in spirit is to pray for and with each other.

Ask your spouse what prayer requests he /she has and then record them in a journal. It is faith-building to look back and see God's marvelous answers. So many are frustrated because their spouse does not meet their spiritual expectations. Surrender your expectations and begin to pray the Word. You will always be praying in the perfect will of God. Too often we tell our spouse our frustrations when we need to tell the Lord.

Pray these verses of scripture for your spouse and yourself:

- Colossians 1:9-14
- Romans 15:13
- Philippians 1:6

- Psalm 121
- I Corinthians 1:4-8

14. Leadership/conviction for family

"And if it seem evil unto you to serve the LORD, choose you this day whom ye will serve; whether the gods which your fathers served that were on the other side of the flood, or the gods of the Amorites, in whose land ye dwell: but as for me and my house, we will serve the LORD" (Joshua 24:15).

Pray this verse the following way:

"Lord, help me to make a conscious decision every day to serve You—that I will not serve the gods of the world or continue ungodly traditions that have been passed down through my family, but that I will, along with my entire household, serve You with a sincere heart."

- II Timothy 3:14-15
- Titus 1:9
- Ephesians 5:22-26, 28
- Proverbs 3:13
- Proverbs 3:21-24
- Psalm 25:4-5

15. Protection

"When thou passest through the waters, I will be with thee; and through the rivers, they shall not overflow thee: when thou walkest through the fire, thou shalt not be burned; neither shall the flame kindle upon thee" (Isaiah 43:2).

Pray this:

> "Lord, no matter my circumstance or the trials, help me to understand that Your Word has great and precious promises, and that You are faithful and will fulfill Your Word. Let me realize there is nothing that comes against me that will be greater than the power of Your Spirit that guides me. Help me to study the lives of those in Your Word that suffered and yet were not dismayed, to understand that You are the Master of all situations and will uphold me so that I will not lose my trust and faith in You."

Search out other Scripture passages for whatever is happening in your life. Use them for a shield from the experiences you will face.

- Deuteronomy 31:8
- II Thessalonians 3:3
- Psalm 121:8
- Isaiah 54:17
- I Chronicles 4:10
- Isaiah 41:10

16. Godly example in the workplace

"Blessed is the man that walketh not in the counsel of the ungodly, nor standeth in the way of sinners, nor sitteth in the seat of the scornful. But his delight is in the law of the LORD; and in his law doth he meditate day and night. And he shall be like a tree planted by the rivers of water, that bringeth forth his fruit in his season; his leaf also shall not wither; and whatsoever he doeth shall prosper" (Psalm 1:1-3).

Pray the above verse this way:

> "Heavenly Father, guide my steps that I will not walk in the way of an ungodly man or heed his council, that I will not lean toward the way of sinners, or become scornful no matter the circumstances I deal with. Help me to delight in your law and be a happy Christian meditating on You and Your Word rather than on the things the ungodly do and say. Help me to stand apart from their ways while still loving their souls, and be a godly example to them at all times."

Pray that you will fulfill the following verses in your lifestyle as you deal with co-workers and employers.

- Psalm 128:1-2
- Proverbs 3:5-10
- Proverbs 18:15-16
- Matthew 5:14-16
- Romans 12:16-18, 21
- Ephesians 6:5-8

17.   Cleansing the home

Psalm 101 was written when David brought the ark of God back to Jerusalem. It had been gone for almost a century. David realized preparation had to be made for this important event. He was willing to do whatever was necessary for the presence of God to inhabit the house of Israel. This psalm is a pattern to cleanse your own home so the presence of God can dwell there.

Read the chapter and then pray the verses in your own words.

18. Seeking after God

"Seek ye the LORD while he may be found, call ye upon him while he is near"(Isaiah 55:6).

Look up and pray the following verses.

- Acts 17:27
- Ephesians 1:17-19
- Colossians 1:9-11

19. Spiritual maturity

"Brethren, be not children in understanding: howbeit in malice be ye children, but in understanding be men" (I Corinthians 14:20).

- Philippians 1:6
- I Thessalonians 5:23
- Psalm 119:11
- Psalm 27:5
- Proverbs 4:11-12
- Deuteronomy 33:27

Portions of this chapter are adapted from *Praying the Word Effectively*, compiled by Linda Gleason, © 2004, Word Aflame Press, Hazelwood, MO 63042-2299. Used by permission.

God's Precious Promises
He Offers Them to Each of Us!

"Whereby are given unto us exceeding great and precious promises ..." (II Peter 1:4).

The Bible is full of promises we can apply to our daily lives. When we fail to believe God's Word, we live below our privileges. Filling our hearts and minds with His Word every day develops our spiritual muscles.

"These words are true and faithful" (Revelation 21:5).

Although we may doubt our worth, God loved us enough to die for us. (See John 3:16.) He desires to spend eternity with us. In addition, He gives us hope for this life too.

"For I know the thoughts that I think toward you, says the LORD, thoughts of peace and not of evil, to give you a future and a hope" (Jeremiah 29:11, NKJV).

Below are just a few of the promises of God found in His Word:

Comfort

- "I will not leave you comfortless: I will come to you" (John 14:18).

Direction

- "And thine ears shall hear a word behind thee, saying, This is the way, walk ye in it, when ye turn to the right hand, and when ye turn to the left" (Isaiah 30:21).

- "In all thy ways acknowledge him, and he shall direct thy paths" (Proverbs 3:6).

Encouragement

- "Cast thy burden upon the Lord, and he shall sustain thee: he shall never suffer the righteous to be moved" (Psalm 55:22).

- "The Lord is on my side; I will not fear: what can man do unto me?" (Psalm 118:6).

- "The Lord is good, a strong hold in the day of trouble; and he knoweth them that trust in him" (Nahum 1:7).

Fear

- "For God hath not given us the spirit of fear; but of power, and of love, and of a sound mind" (II Timothy 1:7).

- "Fear thou not; for I am with thee: be not dismayed; for I am thy God: I will strengthen thee; yea, I will help thee" (Isaiah 41:10).

Forgiveness

- "And whenever you stand praying, if you have anything against anyone, forgive him, that your Father in heaven may also forgive you your trespasses. But if you do not forgive, neither will your Father in heaven forgive your trespasses" (Mark 11:25-26, NKJV).

- "Judge not, and ye shall not be judged: condemn not, and ye shall not be condemned: forgive, and ye shall be forgiven" (Luke 6:37).

Healing

- "But he was wounded for our transgressions, he was bruised for our iniquities: the chastisement of our peace was upon him; and with his stripes we are healed" (Isaiah 53:5).

- "And the Lord will take away from thee all sickness, and will put none of the evil diseases ... upon thee" (Deuteronomy 7:15).

- "For I will restore health unto thee, and I will heal thee of thy wounds, saith the Lᴏʀᴅ" (Jeremiah 30:17).

Help

- "But I am poor and needy; yet the Lord thinketh upon me: thou art my help and my deliverer" (Psalm 40:17).

- "God is our refuge and strength, a very present help in trouble" (Psalm 46:1).

Hope

- "Happy is he that hath the God of Jacob for his help, whose hope is in the Lᴏʀᴅ his God" (Psalm 146:5).

- "The steps of a good man are ordered by the Lᴏʀᴅ, and He delights in his way. Though he fall, he shall not be utterly cast down; for the Lᴏʀᴅ upholds him with His hand" (Psalm 37:23-24, NKJV).

Identity

- "And will be a Father unto you, and ye shall be my sons and daughters, saith the Lord Almighty" (II Corinthians 6:18).

- "I know thee by name" (Exodus 33:17).

Joy

- "In thy presence is fulness of joy" (Psalm 16:11).

- "Yet I will rejoice in the LORD, I will joy in the God of my salvation" (Habakkuk 3:18).

- "They shall obtain gladness and joy; and sorrow and mourning shall flee away" (Isaiah 51:11).

Peace

- "Be careful [anxious] for nothing; but in every thing by prayer and supplication with thanksgiving let your requests be made known unto God. And the peace of God, which passeth all understanding, shall keep your hearts and minds through Christ Jesus" (Philippians 4:6-7).

- "Peace I leave with you, My peace I give to you; not as the world gives do I give to you. Let not your heart be troubled, neither let it be afraid" (John 14:27, NKJV).

Prayer

- "Blessed be God, who has not turned away my prayer, nor His mercy from me!" (Psalm 66:20, NKJV).

- "And it shall come to pass, that before they call, I will answer; and while they are yet speaking, I will hear" (Isaiah 65:24).

Protection

- "The name of the LORD is a strong tower: the righteous runneth into it, and is safe" (Proverbs 18:10).

- "And thou shalt be secure, because there is hope ... and thou shalt take thy rest in safety. Also thou shalt lie down, and none shall make thee afraid" (Job 11:18-19).

- "The LORD shall preserve thee from all evil: he shall preserve thy soul. The LORD shall preserve thy going out and thy coming in" (Psalm 121:7-8).

- "Fear ye not, stand still, and see the salvation of the LORD. ... The LORD shall fight for you, and ye shall hold your peace" (Exodus 14:13-14).

- "No weapon formed against you shall prosper, and every tongue which rises against you in judgment you shall condemn. This is the heritage of the servants of the LORD, and their righteousness is from Me,' says the LORD" (Isaiah 54:17, NKJV).

- "When the enemy shall come in like a flood, the Spirit of the LORD shall lift up a standard against him" (Isaiah 59:19).

Provision

- "I have been young, and now am old; yet have I not seen the righteous forsaken, nor his seed begging bread" (Psalm 37:25).

- "The LORD is my shepherd; I shall not want" (Psalm 23:1).

Reassurance

- "I will never leave thee, nor forsake thee" (Hebrews 13:5).

- "Lo, I am with you alway, even unto the end of the world" (Matthew 28:20).

- "These things I have spoken to you, that in Me you may have peace. In the world you will have tribulation; but be of good cheer, I have overcome the world" (John 16:33, NKJV).

Strength

- "The LORD will give strength unto his people" (Psalm 29:11).

- "But they that wait upon the LORD shall renew their strength; they shall mount up with wings as eagles; they shall run, and not be weary; and they shall walk, and not faint" (Isaiah 40:31).

- "My grace is sufficient for thee: for my strength is made perfect in weakness" (II Corinthians 12:9).

Temptation

- "There hath no temptation taken you but such as is common to man: but God is faithful, who will not suffer you to be tempted above that ye are able; but will with the temptation also make a way to escape, that ye may be able to bear it." (I Corinthians 10:13).

Wisdom

- "If any of you lack wisdom, let him ask of God ... and it shall be given him" (James 1:5).

Key Points:

- Prayer combined with God's Word will give us victory in the situations of life.

- There is nothing too big or too small to bring before God.

- God keeps His promises. His Word is true.